T0120581

Grab a cup of
COFFEE
or
A GLASS
"new"
WINE

It's
Testimony Time...

Kirsten Alexis McKenley

WESTBOW
PRESS®
A DIVISION OF THOMAS NELSON
& ZONDERVAN

This book is a work of non-fiction. Unless otherwise noted, the author
and the publisher make no explicit guarantees as to the accuracy of
the information contained in this book and in some cases, names of
people and places have been altered to protect their privacy.

WestBow Press books may be ordered through booksellers or by contacting:

WestBow Press
A Division of Thomas Nelson & Zondervan
1663 Liberty Drive
Bloomington, IN 47403
www.westbowpress.com
844-714-3454

Because of the dynamic nature of the Internet, any web addresses or
links contained in this book may have changed since publication and
may no longer be valid. The views expressed in this work are solely those
of the author and do not necessarily reflect the views of the publisher,
and the publisher hereby disclaims any responsibility for them.

Any people depicted in stock imagery provided by Getty Images are
models, and such images are being used for illustrative purposes only.
Certain stock imagery © Getty Images.

Scripture taken from the New King James Version®. Copyright © 1982
by Thomas Nelson. Used by permission. All rights reserved.

ISBN: 978-1-6642-4070-4 (sc)
ISBN: 978-1-6642-4069-8 (e)

Print information available on the last page.

WestBow Press rev. date: 7/22/2021

Contents

Dedication

Testimony time dedicated to my beloved Aunt Viola Manning. She was an integral part of my life when I needed true agape love.

Simply put she was the essence of the meaning "the simple gospel of Jesus Christ".

Always serving, hospitable and loving me as if I was the only person in the world, I needed that, specifically at that time. The time I speak about, were my formative years, my life fragmented in many different parts and only the unfailing love of Jesus Christ could heal.

Her simplicity and love of the word and work of the Lord has no doubt led me to the walk in Christ that I now have today.

Her life was not perfect, my life is not perfect but she showed me…

Perfected love.

HONOR

Today I honor my parents Herb and Ruth who are both in heaven now. They are my parents sacred and secure, insulated in the pavilion of my heart.

I love you Mommy and Daddy.

PSALM 91

He who dwells in the secret place of the Most High shall abide under the shadow of the Almighty. I will say of the Lord "He is my refuge and my fortress: My God, in Him I will trust."

Surely He shall deliver you from the snare of the fowler and from the perilous pestilence.

He shall cover you with His feathers and under His wings you shall take refuge;

His truth shall be your shield and buckler. You shall not be afraid of the terror by night, nor of the arrow that flies by day, nor of the pestilence that walks in darkness, nor of the destruction that lays waste at noonday.

A thousand may fall at your side, and ten thousand at your right hand but it shall not come near you. Only with your eyes shall you look and see the reward of the wicked.

Because you have made the LORD, who is my refuge, even the Most High, your dwelling place, no evil shall befall you, nor shall any plague come near your dwelling;

For He shall give His angels charge over you, to keep you in all your ways. In their hands they shall bear you up, lest you dash your foot against a stone. You shall tread upon the Lion and the cobra, the young lion and the serpent you shall trample underfoot. Because He has set his love upon Me, therefore I will deliver him; I will set him on high, because he has known My name.

He shall call upon Me, and I will answer him; I shall be with him in trouble; I will deliver him and honor him. With Long life I shall satisfy him.

And show him My salvation.

PSALM 91: 1-16
The Holy Bible;
New King James Version

…my favorite psalm

preface

This little book is about the Testimonies that I have had the pleasure of living throughout these 62 years of my life.

The word of God says:

> **"And they overcame him by the blood of the lamb and by the word of their testimony, and they did not love their lives to the death.**
> **Revelation 12:11**

The Holy Bible
New King James Version

I take this verse very seriously, as it has led me to many victories. I have learned to decree and declare it over my life. I have become an overcomer, and am always growing and healing and learning how to **live** *as an overcomer.*

It has been difficult, at times, as people (especially in the body of Christ) see you going through something, whatever it may be, tragic or not and they immediately think you did something wrong, God doesn't love you, you are a bad person, or whatever they may come up with.

I know...because I used to be one of those people.

Yes, we are all guilty of carnal thinking, myself included. But God, has been gracious to me spanked me with His big fat frying pan in the Heavenly kitchen up there, and knocked some sense into my stubborn head. **"Judge not."** He would say to me...stubborn little rascal that I was. I wouldn't listen so He knocked me out cold at times.

I know some think God would not do that what kind of God does *she* serve? Well, the same God you do, the one that ***Disciplines those that He loves.*** Thank God He *loves* me, and He loves me a lot!

But..

With His helping hand, I got up, dusted myself off and kept going ***WITH HIM*** leading the way.

Safer!

Writing this book has been a wonderful experience as I continue to grow in the Lord, becoming healthy, forgiving easier, which has lead me to be happier. This happiness, I must explain, is not the kind of happiness that comes because everything is going *TRIUMPHANTLY* in my life.

It is the happiness that abides in, and built on, the **Joy of the Lord** kind of happiness.

I have been adopted and grafted into the True Vine, the Kingdom of God culture of Righteousness, Peace and Joy in the Holy Ghost. I understand it and am grateful that God has chosen me for whatever it is He has chosen me for. I am happy, glad and grateful that I have reached to that place, in my life, where I can say that truthfully.

He trusts me now with the dreams I have had for years. The purging and pruning process to have me established in Him was long, winding, and, at times, for me, brutal. But it was necessary to have me at the place where I could become established in Him.

I remember I received a prophetic word about a dream I have had since I was four years old. The dream started off well, but then, it died. I became so entrenched with the Lord I forgot about the dream and just FELL deeply and madly in love with Jesus...as the desires of this world began to fade away as I grew more deeply in love with Him.

When the prophetic word was spoken over me, I almost rejected it and spit it out because I was not really interested in it any more. This dream was **"HUGE"**. For me to have forgotten it was just simply ludicrous, but I did forget about it. The Holy Ghost said "no, don't dismiss it, the dream came from me, now I can trust you"

and ...
now Jesus...
I trust you!

Testimony

..Sometimes when we make choices and in the sincerity of our hearts believe it is the right choice, it may not turn out the way you expect. hasn't for me, however, it has always allowed me to bloom and blossom in ways I never saw or knew. such is the case with K VINAIGRETTE.

I went to Germany in 1983 to dance and be a part of a singing trio of women, my girlfriend and college best friend, Jyl, were there together working under and with a producer who was extremely talented. we each had HUGE dreams of making it under his leadership and guidance, he was a Mozart of his time, able to write, produce songs working for 13-16 hour periods at a time w/o ceasing, with ease. passionate and intense.

Jyl and I were dancers and singers backing up his wife the solo/ principal singer of the group. I remember I choreographed 17 pieces of choreography in 9 months, one day I spent 5 hours on one piece "fire" that he had written the score for, Jyl, I believe, wrote the lyrics. The song moved me to no end and I had to dance, I had to choreograph to it, I HAD TO move...I WAS ON FIRE! I completed the piece. Exhausted but happy. Thus was the case of dancing, working every day on this album as we got ready to promote it and take it to the record labels, I remember being in the rooms with EMI record label producers and they were all speaking in German about the work/s we had done so far and their sincere interest in it. I did not understand a WORD they were saying, but read their body language for truth, being a dancer that part of it came naturally for me. I learnt how to watch, this continued for several months along with going on the road to promote the album. At some point during all this we had to eat.

I enjoy salads and love making them and eating all of them. Jyl gave me a little insight as to the foundational making of a salad dressing, the producer's sister had taught her so she passed the info unto me. I ran with it to make a long story short, and would make the salad dressing every night, simple: oil, vinegar, lemon, mustard, and scallions. Besides they HATED the way I made coffee, the nerve of them! I love coffee I am from Jamaica and we have the best coffee!

I moved back to NYC because things did not work out AT ALL in Germany, almost tragic, near misses ALL OF THE ABOVE. as Helen Baylor says in her "testimony" ..."but I had a praying grandmother", I had a "praying auntie" (ma vie)...and a risen Savior, who by the way lives now to make intercession for us. I made it back safely (physically) to NYC in tears, ruin and in failure

.....so I thought.

.....fast forward, continued making and also developing the dressing adding and subtracting oils, vinegars and different ingredients... presenting it at my little dinner parties etc.....everyone LOVED IT. Wow imagine that. " bottle it" they told me. never thought of that...being right brained and ONLY creative, not a business bone in my body...no way. HE MAKES A WAY WHERE THERE IS "NO WAY".

I bottled it. KVINAIGRETTE.COM.

Oh...the dancing and choreography? Whatever became of that piece of the puzzle that is what I went to Germany for in the first place... what happened there?

Well I learnt to choreograph to "commercial" music, and with that piece of information I wrote directed, choreographed and staged a Gospel Musical called "Tribute to Jesus"

It was premiered at my church after 2 years of rehearsals bringing over 400 souls to the altar, in repentance, and re dedication to the Lord including my beloved father, Herb, my sweet sister Laura, her son Jason, my favorite nephew, and my darling son Adam, still little at the time. HE climbed up on to the stage just to give me a hug.

"Mommy, can we go home now?"

Now, he is saved, on fire, and married with a family, his testimony...

POWERFUL.

Beloved, keep running, keep dreaming, keep on hoping, keep on moving ...there is a "yes" out there somewhere, for you, you just have to find it!

I did!

Sandra Price, thank you for encouraging me to write this piece... you are

"Priceless"

And we know that all things work together for good to those who love God, to those who are the called according to His purpose.

Romans 8: 28
New King James Version.
My favorite scriptural address.

1

MY Destiny Begins

1963...   I was 4 years old.

Kirsten: Marlene!

Marlene: Yes Kirsten!

Kirsten: Can you make me look as pretty as those women in that magazine....

Marlene: At 8:O'Clock Kirsten at 8:O'Clock....

Kirsten: What does 8:O'Clock look like?

Marlene: When the short hand reaches 8 and the long hand on the clock reaches 12.
Then...it is 8:O'Clock.

I sat in front of the little clock with my little hands and fingers cupped under my chin to wait for ...

8 O' Clock.

My destiny begins....

*   *   *

2

God answers itzzy bitzy prayers...

1968-9... or somewhere around that time, I was about 8-9 years old maybe 10 or 11...who knows!

Anyway... I was taking a much required examination in my prep school run by Nuns!

CATHOLIC.

VERY STRICK.

Well, unfortunately for me, I didn't study for the examination soo I came up with another solution, a plan..

Cheat.

K..

So I was seated at my desk with the test on my left and the book with *ALL* the answers on my right. There I was cheating away... something, frankly, I am not good at, not because I am miss goodie two shoe or anything, but just had not cheated before so I was simply doing it openly and the only way I knew how.. *honestly!*

CHEATING!!

I was on a roll..woo hoo!!

DON'T ASK!

Got caught by the teacher!

She promptly sent me down to see the Head Mistress.

A NUN!

Oh no

It is over!

Thank fully there was a line at her front door so I joined the line.

k... that gave me a few minutes to devise a plan.

pray.

Only prayer would get me out of this one. I started with the

"Our Father"... prayer

Forgot the words not good.

Tried counting the rosary…

Pitched those string of beads over my shoulder the line is getting shorter, and my plan is NOT WORKING!

Messy!

Sweating bullets as the line in front of the headmistress office is getting shorter and shorter… too fast for me to get my prayer into Heaven..

Cute little damsel, with two pigtails, in damsel in distress mode.

Finally, it is over.

Standing in front of her, the NUN of all NUNS she was standing up behind her desk with a frown on her face.

"McKenley? What is it?" she said.

"Never mind…I have an errand for you to run for me"

HALLELUJAH! My little mind BELTED out.

THANK YOU FATHER!

I could tell she was exhausted with everyone who was there before me, no doubt answering questions…or giving her advice, or handing down JUDGEMENTS on those that were in line before me.

"Yes Sister Martinella!

"Please run to the Music Director and give her this message."

"Yes Sister Martinella"

Her office was at the other end of the school where the back gate of the school was located ...all my school friends saw me running as fast as I could to get the message to the music director. They thought I had been expelled as they were looking though the classroom window. I guess by this time they all knew I had been sent to the headmistress' office for cheating.

I just wanted to redeem myself man...who cares what THEY thought!

So I delivered the message and ran all the way back to Sister Martinella's office.

By this time I am sweating for two reasons.

Running as fast as I could back and forth to deliver a message...

... and now the HORRIFYING task of having to tell the Head Mistress,

A NUN, why I had been at her office door in the first place. This is disastrous at best, this lying cheating bit, what a horror, never again, I will fail any day of the week, better than triumphantly cheating!

"I delivered the message Sister Martinella"

My father is going to kill me …and Sister Martinella is going to turn me upside down and shake every bit of dishonesty left inside of me.

A TKO moment (technical knockout)..

…but that didn't happen.

She told me to go back to my class room and to never do whatever it was that I did.

GOD

ANSWERES

Itzy bitzy

PRAYERS!

Oh..that's right

I didn't even have to pray...

Wow!

3

Summer Of 1977

The year I got saved, I was 18 years old.

The summer of 1977 was spent in NYC with my aunt and two brothers, we each had summer jobs so we were all very busy, and had something to do for the summer before going back to college.

My days were filled. I got up at 6 AM took the train to Harlem where I taught inner city kids, dance from 8 AM to about 3 PM. I would then head to the Alvin Ailey School of Dance to take dance classes that lasted up until 8 – 9 PM, then cleaned toilet bowls/janitorial (with my leotards on), as part of my work scholarship program.

Loved every minute of it. I would get home at about 11 PM at night, repeating the same thing over each day for 8 weeks. I was exhausted but felt and knew I was accomplishing something. I didn't know at the time, what God was weaving in me, but I was happy and fulfilled!

During my days in Harlem I would sit on one of the benches and have my little sandwich for lunch, I met a sweet young man with a tiny "green" bible. He would talk to me about Jesus, which was easy for me to grasp, as I was catholic and went to a catholic prep and high school in Jamaica.

He was not pushy at all and I felt safe...for some reason I HAVE to feel safe, even now...if I do not, it is a "now you see me now you don't" moment...

Anyway, we became friends and he would explain bible verses to me as I asked questions. He introduced me to his sisters "girlfriends" from his church and they were nice, fun and definitely had a thriving relationship with Jesus.

Then came the day when I went to church with them!

It was a Pentecostal church, HUGE in the swaying movements of the Holy Ghost...what did I know!

I just knew I was waiting to hear about giving my life to Jesus, something along those lines, I was listening intently...A deer in headlines moment...

Then came the "question"....

"Is there anyone here that wants to give their life to Jesus?"

..finally!

I shot up like an arrow! I was dressed in this beautiful red dress, just for the occasion... and walked down the aisle all alone, apparently everyone else had given their life to Jesus, so I was alone on that little "runway".

I got in front of this Preacher man with BEADS of sweat running down his face.

"Do you want to *die* for Jesus" he asked

"What? Die?" No! Now I was utterly confused.

"No… the boy with the "little green" bible told me to *Give my life to Jesus*

"Not die"

…I am only 18???!!!

Wrong church!

Where is that little chap? Nowhere around.

I am now battling it out with Jesus as they wrapped me up in white garments and promptly "deposited me in a pool water.

Baptism.

I left the church in tears…clueless as to what had happened, but strangely enough I still felt "safe".

I got home wet from top to bottom in my little red dress. But…

SAVED.

That was 44 years ago and I have come to realize that yes the Preacher man was right.

I did *"die"* that day, and was *"born again"* at the same time.

It was the greatest day of my life!

4

1983

I moved to Germany to become a Huge Star. I was invited by a college friend to come over there to be a part of a trio made up of two dancers and a solo singer. I choreographed seventeen pieces of work along with writing the Lyrics to a song. We traveled throughout Germany presenting our product which created a lot of buzz. Things looked good as EMI and other record companies were very interested.

The plan went south when all fell apart because of circumstances beyond my control. I left **DEVASTED** crying on the TWA flight back to NYC ...I had failed, I was only 25 years old at the time and thought I had gotten a HUGE BREAK.

I came back to NYC went back to work for the same Restaurant to make money and make a living...the one I was accustomed to.

...I had learned, however, to make Salad dressing whilst living in Germany, I later bottled that dressing now called **K VINAIGRETTE.**

Whilst I was there,

I learned that commercial music was a four beat count, I choreographed seventeen pieces of choreography whilst I was there, to no avail.

In 1986 I rededicated my life back to the LORD. In 1997-99 I wrote, choreographed, directed and produced a play called **Tribute to Jesus, it took two years to complete it.** I began that play with two dancers, when we premiered it at the church of which I was then a member, the size of the production company had grown from 2 dancers to over 150 singers, dancers, actors, and musicians and it was performed before five thousand people.

It was on a Wednesday evening and four hundred souls came forward to give or rededicate their lives to the Lord.

I NEVER KNEW...I NEVER KNEW that God would use the salad dressing that I learned to make whilst living in Germany into a salad dressing line, and use the information that I received about choreography to create a gospel musical to honor Him...SAVING SOULS....

I NEVER KNEW.

5

The audition

In the spring of 1977 a fellow classmate/dancer friend of mine at the North Carolina School of Arts asked me...

"Hey Kirsten what are you doing this summer?" I told her I would be in NYC for the summer, she suggested that the Alvin Ailey School of Dance would be a great place for me to be for the summer.

She explained that they usually had a Summer scholarship program and that she thought I would get one!!

....so I went ...to the Alvin Ailey School of Dance Summer Scholarship "audition."

I was eighteen years old and afraid not knowing what to expect... the amount of dancers auditioning that day totaled approximately 700 to 800 girls and boys. We were standing in line in the hot, humid sun taking up three to four city blocks in New York City.

I was a little deer in headlights!

Well finally they called my number and I auditioned after waiting in line for about 2-3 hours...standing... waiting....in the sun. I went into the sweaty dance studio where ballet was the first step to the audition process. Ballet was not my strong suit, even though I had beautiful "ballet feet", my strong point was modern dance...not ballet.

I got eliminated immediately after 5 minutes.

...DEVASTATED...

No time for tears..

...I went down stairs to the holding room..

Waited and hoped beyond measure for another 10 hours, praying that maybe...just maybe.

....I could not leave ....

I did not leave until the very last person had auditioned...

..I took the train home and then the bus. Got home at 11:00 PM that evening...

Wept.

Next day...

...looked through the yellow pages (remember *those* pages) to find another dance school giving auditions

...found one.

My hand went to the phone to call the number, a rotary phone, a landline phone... remember those phones?

..My phone starting ringing...I answered it.

..."Hello" ...

"May I speak to Kirsten please?"...

"This is Kirsten".

"Hi Kirsten this is Kermit from the Alvin Ailey School of Dance"...

"OH!"

"Hello!??"

"Kirsten we are calling to tell you that we made a mistake in your auditioning with us at Ailey, and in fact, you are being offered a Dance Scholarship for the summer."

I started to laugh to myself..."NO" you did not make a mistake (I thought) literally laughing to myself...I *am horrible* at ballet! Have beautiful feet though!

Then I realized he was **SERIOUS.**

He continued....

"The only scholarships that we have available, however, are work scholarships" ....

"Janitorial...cleaning the toilets after classes...."

I accepted with absolute glee!

Danced on Scholarship

Cleaned the toilet bowls...

in the summer of 1977 at the Alvin Ailey School of Dance in New York City...

..No big deal!

They invited me back for a full year to remain on **full** scholarship there....however I went back to North Carolina School of the Performing Arts where there was a scholarship waiting for me ....

God's favor, and His grace toward me, He had two scholarships for me in one school year.

He gave me a choice.

HE is the Best Ever!

27 YEARS LATER...

2004..

Visiting my Father in the Hospital...he was dying... spending 10 days with him,

By his bedside.

One of my girlfriends called on me to ask how my Father was doing and mentioned that a mutual friend of ours Tony/Dancer, was in the hospital as well, and underwent minor surgery and that he was in the room close to my Father. As she was speaking... the Holy Spirit was speaking to me in my *other* "ear" that it was Tony...it was Tony....

I blurted out ..." **It was Tony**"!!....

..It was Tony that spoke up for me *that day* at the Alvin Ailey School of Dance Audition and asked them to give me another chance! I saw in one

"heavenly Glimpse" as the Holy Ghost downloaded that revelation to me from the "Throne Room", some 27 years later....

...needless to say my girlfriend was clue less as what on earth I was talking about...

.."it was Tony...it was Tony..."thankfully she is my oldest and most cherished friend, Michele, of over 55 years … so she knew how silly I could be at times...so she just ignored the..

"it was Tony…it was Tony" moment.

That morning I was walking into the hospital to spend the day with my Father, as I entered the hospital I came face to face, physically, with

...Tony...

He was leaving the hospital.... the double glass doors separated us, we looked at each other eyeball to eyeball.

The doors opened and I said to him …

"I am Kirsten McKenley, do you remember me?"

"yes" he said.

I asked him if it was he that put in a good word for me at the Alvin Ailey school of Dance in the summer of 1977?

"yes" he said.

I hugged him and thanked him, and told him that I created a theatrical musical called

"Tribute to Jesus" based on what he did for me that day in 1977, and the testimony of it bringing over 400 souls to the Altar of the Lord in Salvation and re dedication....

In the year 2007 I wrote the screenplay based on the theatrical production of *"Tribute to Jesus"*

"And we know that all things work together for good to those who love God, to those who are the called according to His purpose"

Romans 8:28

New King James Version

Yes.. I know I used this scriptural verse before in this book of testimonies.

It is my favorite scripture and worth repeating, so there!

*   *   *

My daddy...

He did not die...then...but lived....

...is it 8 O'clock yet...

2007... Forgiving.

The week my daddy died.

November 26, 2007

I had just completed writing a screenplay at the Library and was on the phone with my beloved sister Laura, just talking about Daddy and his failing health, he was in the hospital. We were both discussing his life, legacy and his love, hoping that he would be able to "hold on" for a little longer. We ended the conversation by saying this..

"His Mission here on earth was accomplished"

My phone rang less than 5 minutes later, her number popped up on the screen.

I knew.

Daddy died.

Cried.

I asked God... "how do I transition from tonight to tomorrow morning..?" I have never had a day without my daddy in it, I knew he was in Heaven. I KNEW IT!... but it was going to be an interesting night, that's for sure! God told me to put in some DVD tapes of his Olympic legacy, in which I would hear his voice as I slept.

I did. I woke up the next morning with an "open heaven" over my head and

"joy" in my heart.

Daddy was safe and sound in the Heaven.

The sun was shining, literally. It was a beautiful sun shinny day, physically.

Transition was perfect. He is forever alive in a sacred place in my heart.

ALIVE.

...

Now came the daunting task of renewing my US Passport in time for his going home celebration... in Jamaica, His beloved homeland.

Jamaica gave him an "official funeral." Burying him at our "National Heroes Park", where only our National Heroes and Prime Ministers are buried. He is neither, He is a **National Treasure**.... Beloved by all. He is the last person that will be buried there. An official decision made by the Jamaican Government.

I am humbled and honored to have had him as my father in this life...

He was a walking epistle...never saw him with a bible, a good Samaritan, once helping a beloved friend of ours who had undergone a nervous breakdown to live in our home until he got well...at **NO** charge. Our family made room for this person as he healed. At the home going and celebration of the life of my father, some 50 years later, he came up to me to say hello. "How are you? I asked.

"I am well I am well, I am married now and I live in Rome, Italy. When I heard that Herb had died I had to come to say "goodbye" to my good friend.

...tears falling.

Getting my US Passport in time ...I had ten days...

I knew a friend who could make it possible for me to get this done in a timely manner. She knew a State Senator and got his office to do the impossible for me. In the process of doing so there was a blockage, a slowing down of movement, extremely frustrating as I was running out of time.

One night I was watching television and listening to the pastor of a church talk about *forgiveness.*

There was someone in my life that I had not forgiven, unfortunately, as hard as I tried to forgive, it was difficult, to say the least. In obedience, I stretched my hand towards my roommate and asked her to agree with me in prayer in forgiving this person.

No lightning bulbs crashed and burned nothing significant happened. Just an act...I did not "feel a thing." Being obedient.

The next morning, huge movement happened with my passport, the "locater" number that they were waiting on was located and the process continued.

There was still some blockage and I became agitated as I continued to wait.

I asked God in prayer, "Would you allow the person who is typing up my passport to call me please?"

Now, there is no access in or out of the passport office by employees or applicants,

Fort Knox!

…who knows, who cares… **"God YOU are God and YOU can get in…"** I need Your access.

A day later…

Ring, ring, ring.

"Hello"

"May I speak to Kirsten, please?"

"This is she"

"Hi Kirsten this is Linda inside the passport office in Hart Fort Connecticut, I am sorry to hear about your father, I am typing up your passport for you now, I want to get this out to you as quickly as possible"

"Thank you!" I said.

She knew about my father…because the Lord had the State Senator's office personally handle EVERTHING for me. God is great. He is a very present help in the time of trouble. I love Him so very much. My Heart belongs to Him.

I received the passport the next day at 8:30 in the morning, by federal express.

The passport office paid for the shipping.

Access …

Granted.

I learnt many things during this brief episode of saying goodbye to my father, the chief of which was the blessing of forgiveness, as I learnt how to be obedient to forgive, and, not to wait the an emotional feeling.

A quality of which my father had a double portion.

7

God's Goodness

I was in the employ of a bank over 25 years ago and making very little money, struggling at best. Raising my son as a single parent was financially challenging to say the least. My Father stepped in and asked me to allow him to help, which I did, until I was able to get back on my feet financially.

I got a position as a server in a restaurant to make more money as I had more time on my hands during the evenings. This I did for quite some time. Though I was making more money, I was extremely tired and wanted to quit my "other" job...as a server and just stick with my more permanent job at the bank. I kept getting a nudge from the Holy Ghost to just stick with the server position...He would give me strength.

My supervisor at the bank *needed* and wanted Salvation. To cut a long story short I took her into the ladies' room one day and prayed the prayer of Salvation with her ...banged her head with a "heavenly frying pan"

...led her to Christ!

Whew!

Thank You Father! Enough said!

...any way back to my story...

Some weeks later, after work, at about 4 PM, I, along with approximately ten to twelve employees attended a meeting in the conference room. No idea why. We were laid off due to the financial recession the country was in at the time. I believe I was the only one in that room that had "another" job though it was part time it was still a job, even though I was only a "server" in a restaurant ... it was still earning extra money.

My supervisor (who I led to Christ) knew the situation ahead of time was *EXTEMELY* concerned for me. She, apparently, went home the day before this all happened and prayed, for me, with her husband.

She spoke to me after we were all released from the conference room and with tears in her eyes told me how sorry she was and wondered "how are you going to make it?"

It was then, that I told her I had a second job as a server and that it wasn't so bad. She was **RELIEVED** beyond words.!!

I left.

I bawled my eyes out.

I screamed at God and asked Him "why did you let them fire me... WHY?" I was crying all the way home...

It was raining heavily.

Me: I don't care if you don't love me any more God ...I don't care!!! I will always *LOVE* You.

I will never let you go I will **ALWAYS** love you. I am so Mad at you right
Now.

I shouted this to the ONLY HEAVENLY FATHER of the Universe as if *He* were hard of hearing.

I suppose He was crying too as it was raining BUCKETS all the way home. I am not sure if He responded to my madness or not on the expressway... I was screaming at Him... couldn't hear His response, if any.

I finally got home had a couple glasses of wine...calmed down, put on my pinky silky pajamas and felt so much better!....

Hmm...

Went into the restaurant the next evening and told them I was let go from the bank..

GM: Good! Can you work a double tomorrow?
Me: oh...ok!

No one *"cared"* why I got fired or let go, they were just happy to have me full time.

I had incredible favor at that restaurant.

Later, I became General Manager of that restaurant hosting, entertaining and met Movie Stars, Presidents, Princes and Princesses as the General Manager.

God knew the end from the beginning...thank God I hearkened to the nudging of the Holy Ghost to stick it out with the "server" position at that restaurant.

Do you see a man who excels in his work?

He will stand before kings

He will not stand before unknown men.

Proverbs 22: 29

New King James Version

I guess I pleased God...grateful.

...to be serving.

Is it 8 o'clock yet..

The Day I Loved My Enemy and My Enemy Loved Me..

Short but sweet..

Being a restaurant manager can be challenging in many ways especially your employees. I had one such employee.

This employee was extremely rude and insubordinate to me, I promptly fired her! My then GM who actually, that day, was his last day as GM of the restaurant told me to call her back, apologize to her for firing her as I was **NOT** allowed to fire anyone!

I did as I was told. Not happy about it. She apologized too and came back.

She pretty much remained the same as did I. We did not like each other too much, as you can imagine but we both made the best of it.

Several months went by, she was mouthy to me at times...very strong willed little rascal...but then hey...so was I!

One of those times I was pretty tired of the whole thing and simply told her that I loved all my employees even though I knew they all spoke badly about me behind my back. During this little conversation, she actually listened to me and I could see, in her eyes, "revelation" had taken hold of her sweet little heart.

We started to gain a new respect for each other and there was a shifting of respect and honor taking root...in *both* our hearts. A few months maybe weeks later God told me my season was coming to a close there and I should make plans to leave. I found another job, less stressful and gave my notice. She found out and PROMPTLY told me she needed to speak to me.

"What is THIS! I hear you're leaving' ...*where* are you GOING?.." *demanding* little button! How dare I give my notice... and NOT ASK HER PERMISSION FIRST.

I told her what was on my heart, what God had told me to do and that I was following my heart's desire and my dreams. One of my dreams was, indeed, writing this book.

My last day came shortly after wards and I remember standing at the Host stand speaking with my hostesses. She found me and told me, in no uncertain terms, that there was "cookie" at the bar waiting for me!

"What...cookie??" I was mildly confused...

"Come, I'll show you." she said. So I followed behind her like a dutiful manager would do and saw this **BIG** Cookie waiting for me at the bar. It had little yellow flowers squeezed onto it....

I had a yellow blouse that I would wear to work sometimes, she apparently noticed and bought me a big, little "yellow" cookie.

How on God's earth was I going to eat this *BIG* little cookie all by myself.

It was for me she told me **FROM HER**!

Adorable.

I smiled, thanked her, hugged her and took a huge helping of the cookie... hmm delicious. I was moved beyond words and quite frankly wanted to cry.

Later that evening she was leaving work, and I was in the office with two other managers just talking.

She found me and came to say "Goodbye".

We hugged so tight neither one of us wanted to let go. She was a bit taller than me and her arms wrapped around me in a strong hold, as did mine. I kissed her in her ears...you could hear the kiss a mile away. The way I used to kiss my son when he was a baby!

This was a most defining moment of this new season I was about to begin...

God has always given me something to hold unto as I leave one season to go into the next, this was one of those moments. I will NEVER forget my "little" BIG cookie, my precious mouthy employee, of whom I am so proud. She had passed her exams and has now gotten a job in her new field!

Indeed...we are no longer enemies.

Friends.

"But I say to you, love your enemies, bless those who curse you, do good to those who hate you, and pray for those who spitefully use you and persecute you, that you

may be sons of your Father in heaven; for He makes His sun rise on the evil and on the good, and sends rain on the just and on the unjust.

Mathew 5:44-45

New King James Version

This chapter and verse is for me as well...I to have done evil and cursed my enemies and am forever grateful for the everlasting grace and mercy of God.

9

When God Laughs Out Loud...

A few weeks after I rededicated my life to Jesus two beautiful things happened …

within a month I got filled with the abiding presence of the Holy Ghost and I anointed the house where I was living, at the time, with oil.

Let me explain, both were whimsical...if not, laughing out loud moments.

Being filled with the Holy Ghost from the Throne Room.

My sister had herself just received the redemption gift of salvation and so we were back and forth on the phone talking about Jesus.

Well one of the things she told me was to have hands laid on me to get the gift of the Holy Spirit.

The "Holy Spirit" ...what is that? She tried to explain. We were both clueless.

The blind leading the blind moment. She said I had to find an elder with white hair, in the church I was attending and have him lay hands on me... "what is an "elder" with white hair?

Just a clueless little button trying desperately to love God. "Holy Spirit".

"Elder with white hair". "Laying on of hands"...what is *all that about?*

Decided to go to church for Tuesday night service.

I figured God would have it all worked out.

Well He did.

Went to church. Bible in hand.

The preacher man said...

"Well tonight we just going to ask the Holy Spirit to come on down..." I was READY...WOO HOO! Holy Spirit, just as Laura said, she is prophetic, I later found out, so she just spoke out the command... and the rest is history!

THE Holy Spirit! Thank you Jesus! No man with white hair, no elder laying on of hands...just the Holy Ghost... I had no clue where He was going to enter this parade of thoughts that was swirling around in my head and heart. But who cares? He. The Holy Ghost, was on His way and ...I BELIEVED the Preacher man!

k...

The last thing I remembered was just sitting there...yes, a deer in "headlights" moment, waiting ...looking up, down all around for this "Holy Spirit" to show up...

then.............

BOOM, BAM...BOOM SHAKA LAKA...BOOM SHAKA LAKA...........BOOM BOOM.

He came, I was out, hard to describe this on paper, in words...I just know that I was not in the earth realm for an immeasurable amount of time, I was in eternity...I guess...only The Father knows where I galloped off to ..

When I came back I was a wreck, my hat had shifted on my head my ear rings gone, and I was SPEAKING IN SOME UNKNOWN LANGUAGE ...known biblically as tongues, I would later find out. Then I began singing in "tongues" crying my eyeballs out, because I had no clue what had happened, I was all alone in NYC at a church with no real explanation of what was going on inside of me just that it was REAL, different, SAFE.

I asked Jesus in my heart...I felt SAFE with Jesus... "did I get it...did I get it?" .. A lady that was sitting behind me "LAYED" her hands on my right shoulder and said at that precise moment that I asked Jesus if I got it..."just praise Him sista! I did praise Him, galloping off in the "Spirit". The two people that were sitting on either side of me were stiff and stoic, no doubt panicked, as I was having a "moment" or two with Holy Ghost. I guess they didn't get it! Oh well.. They looked really frightened. I guess I must have been carrying on or somethin' they were so stiff... anyway...after the ceremonial blessing and filling of the gift of the Holy Ghost from His Throne Room.... I wept....

God ...

Laughed.

10

When God Laughs at You....

Immediately after I received the Holy Ghost I decided to anoint the house that I lived in. This home, a four story brownstone, belonged to a family friend, and I rented out the basement area. I am not sure if someone had told me about anointing the home or if this word came from the Holy Ghost...but I went to the grocery store and bought 2 large bottles of extra virgin olive oil and started to anoint!

I started at the top of the brownstone, three stories high all the way down to the basement, my floor.

I was EXTREMELY generous with my anointing oil, singing and dancing in the spirit, having a gay old time with the Holy Ghost.

Of course I did this when no one else was home and was very careful not to break anything or touch too many things in each room. I did not know the renter on the top floor so when I went to anoint her upstairs living area I was super careful. Just touching the walls and kitchen area. I was so sure she would want to have the protection of Jesus and the Holy Ghost. Who wouldn't?

Then I anointed the second and third levels where the owner of the house lived. She and I got along very well and she would come to check on me periodically. She was an older lady plump and cheerful...

...think "Aunt Jemima!"

Then came my basement quarters with the winding wooden staircase that lead to where I lived. The basement was very comfortable and I was at total peace there!

So I anointed EVERYTHING with oil. I anointed the winding staircase the kitchen, the bathroom my bedroom...EVERYWHERE! I had an ecstatic time singing as LOUDLY as I could in tongues. Boy what a fabulous sweet time I was having, especially with the staircase, anointing the handles the floor everything.

I had truly captured a part of my life that was missing all along, especially this time around with Jesus. I had just re dedicated my life to him (1986) and now there was new revelation that He was downloading to me at a pace, that was, I thought, faster than the speed of light!

Fast forward a few days later.... Mrs. Bell came down stairs to see me to see how I was doing.

You guessed it!

Remember... think Aunt Jemima!

Me: Mrs. Bell what happened to your knee?!
Mrs. Bell: Chiiiiile! I was coming down the stairs to see you, to
            check on you to see how you were doing, and I just
            tripped and fell down the stairs and when I tried to
            hold on to the handles of the stairs ....I slipped even
            more. ALL that oil ...it was so oily.

"Darlin'"

"I nearly broke my back!"

I nearly fainted!! What do I do now!? Yikes. The woman tripped down the winding staircase on my anointing oil!

Me: Father! Help... what do I say to her, I can't tell her about this anointing thingy. She will think I have lost my mind! *I* don't even know what I was doing... HELP! ...hello! Where are you Father?

God: zzzzzzzzzzzzzzzzzzzzzzzzzzz "silently" laughing out aloud!

Me: Mrs. Bell ...I am SOOOO sorry about your knee!!

(Grasping for words..., beads of holy sweat pouring in and out of me.)

Mrs. Bell: Honey why was there so much oil on the staircase???

At this point, she was now waiting breathlessly for an answer....and staring/glaring at me...

Me: I..I... was coming down the stairs Mrs. Bell, and all this oil was in my hand......and..........and......it......... just.............***FELL OUT!!!***

Mrs. Bell looked at me ......she was utterly confused, "fell out, dear??" she asked. At this point I didn't know ***what*** to say I couldn't tell her the entire truth but I couldn't lie either! Oh no ...I was now saved and completely committed to God, now this. I have an old woman that has now tripped on my anointing oil, and My Heavenly Father was nowhere around...or so I thought!

Later He told me

"Kirsten was laughing so hard at you, and your plight I couldn't answer you, *quite* at that moment!"

God loves us, and, He laughs *AT* us at times simply because He thinks we are funny, confused in a whimsical way, and He knows, in His sovereignty, that all is well.

Is it 8 O'clock yet?

11

Honor thy Mother and Father

"Honor your father and your mother that your days may be long upon the land which the LORD your God is giving you."

Exodus 20:12
New King James Version.

In the 1980's I was living in NYC and began working in the Restaurant Hospitality Business. I was at that time took a position as a server in an exclusive fine dining restaurant on Madison Avenue and 93 Rd Street. I liked the position a lot and enjoyed working there! The owner was nice to me and we had a very small team only 6-7 employees, we all got along.

On one occasion the owner said something to me about one of my parents and quite frankly I was EXTREMELY upset about it and after thinking about it for a day, I quit. I told the owner I didn't like what they said about my Parent and quit immediately.

I was 21 years old.

Walking down Madison Avenue wondering how I was now going to pay my rent was another story!

Though I was saved at the time, I certainly didn't have a thriving relationship with God or Jesus or the Holy Spirit...just saved, that's all!

I certainly did not have any idea about God's promises regarding honoring your Mother and Father...I was just very upset with the owner, I could use another word but I think you get the picture.

I had bought her a cake for that evening's dinner reservations and after thinking about it, I said to her "I didn't like what you said about my Parent, here's your cake, change, receipt and...

"I quit"

"Goodbye"

I had very little experience in the Hospitality industry but decided to stay with it because it was all I knew. I was a dancer, all dancers, musicians, actors, singers went straight to NYC to make it big. I was one of them. Being in the Restaurant Industry as a server, gave me the opportunity to have a very flexible schedule and go on auditions.

As I was walking down Madison Avenue, logic started to *lodge* itself into my brain! How am I going to pay my rent for this/next month?

I walked and walked...ended up in this nightclub at about 2-3 PM in the afternoon wanting to fill out an application.

It was **PITCH BLACK** in there. It was a very exclusive and famous nightclub in NYC,

STUDIO 54. All the very famous and rich movie stars went there, back then, it was the place to be seen.

I thought "oh dear there's no one here," Wait there was someone there! A single man sitting under a single lit lamp...doing nothing.

I walked up to him and asked him for an application for a job. He turned and looked at me and said very clearly and distinctly.

"You don't want to work here, Go to "Windows on the World". I asked him where and what is that?

"That is where you want to work" he said. I asked him where it was he said...

"You can't miss it. It is on top of the tallest building in the world, the most exclusive restaurant in the world, it is in downtown Manhattan"

I walked to the subway, made it to The World Trade Center and took the elevator 107 floors. I was dizzy. All of this happening in one day.

I was able to meet with one of the supervisor's at the time...just happened to be present and got an immediate interview. I told him the whole story of my former employer saying something not so nice about one of my parents, the cake, the receipt and her change...and "goodbye".

He wasn't buying it! He must have thought, I was out of my mind, I looked at him and realized, in his body language, that he wasn't buying my story. I said to him "I could lie to you and *make* up a story ..but I am simply not good at that...so I want to tell you the truth" His entire body language, position, changed and we talked for about thirty minutes. I left and thought, well I gave it my best shot.

It was a Thursday afternoon, I went home and forgot about the whole thing, actually, deciding that I would start my ongoing search for another job the next day, Friday!

On Friday Morning the phone rang.

"Hi May I speak with Kirsten please"

"This is she"

"Hi Kirsten! I am calling from Windows on the World, you interviewed with us yesterday, and you have been hired"

"Please come in on Monday at 10:00 AM sharp to be fitted for your uniform, you must bring beige colored stockings and capezio dance shoes as part of your uniform, Congratulations!"

"Thank You".

Click!

I had the rest of the weekend off!

Hallelujah!

Working at Windows on the World Restaurant was a **GATE,** not a window or a door...but a **GATE** to my entire Restaurant Industry career. It would open doors and windows into other restaurants for me for up to 40 years and still counting. It afforded me the opportunity where companies would create positions for me just on that name alone.

I later realized a few things. The man sitting under the lamp was an angel in human form positioned by God to "direct my steps."

"God watches over His word to perform it." I didn't know all this stuff at 21 years old.

I just wanted a job!

God is Good! Oh by the way, I am good friends with that Supervisor to this day...some 40 years later.

That Night Club, **Studio 54,** held a banquet some years later, for some famous attorney to the Stars.

Windows on the World was asked to do the banquet for them...yep I was on that team. By then, I had become a Captain at **Windows on the World..**

the most exclusive restaurant

..in the world!

God doesn't forget a thing!!!

I am glad I took a stance to honor my beloved parent that day,

With the cake,

The receipt,

The change,

The goodbye.

12

♛

God is faithful

1972/3

One of the world's greatest entertainers of all time was my favorite singer / entertainer.... still is. Well he came to my home country Jamaica and of course I **HAD** to meet him. I dragged my two best girlfriends to come with me to his hotel every day, for the entire time he was in Jamaica...but to no avail, I didn't meet him.

Thirty years later, I was a receptionist with a huge company that represented this world famous entertainer. This person had their own **SOP** system (Standard Operating Procedure). If he called, we DO NOT take a message...he speaks to someone...immediately.

NO EXCEPTIONS.

Well he called one day and I received the call, after doing cartwheels without hands with the other receptionist and having the **NERVE** to put him on hold, I got him through to the correct person and that was that.

I took a deep breath and nodded off into La La Land for about an hour or so.

Unbelievable.

Sometime later, I remembered that thirty years prior I had wanted to and waited anxiously to meet this person, when he came to my homeland. That didn't happen then. But God answered the desire

of my heart, a desire I actually had forgotten about. The other receptionist could have easily gotten the call rollover to her line, instead I received the call. I never met this world famous person, **I SPOKE TO HIM!**

God does NOT forget your dreams...you do, but HE does not! He knows that our desires sometimes are in the hallways of time and we get impatient and loose hope, loose our way and turn away to go back the other way...but His word to you today is TURN AROUND ...face the doorway that will soon open for you. He gives us ALL sign posts to let us know that we ARE going in the right direction

He remembers them and fulfills them for you, to give you hope and a will to HOLD on! He did for me that day.

He is our AMAZING God, Heavenly Father and the lover of our souls.

God is faithful....

13

Obedience is better than sacrice!

One morning after spending some time with God in Prayer I heard a knock on my door. It was someone from the apartment downstairs, she looked a bit upset. She told me she had bumped into my car and wanted to let me know. She was extremely sorry, felt very badly, and was visibly upset.

I asked her if my car had a dent or was just scratched. She said it was just scratched. I told her not to worry, let's go take a look!

She was visibly upset and I immediately felt compassion for her! We both went downstairs to look on the damage...very little! As I was walking downstairs behind her I heard the Lord tell me to "pray" for her. When I saw the damage it was as she said just scratched, no harm done really and I was able to calm her nerves. We took care of the scratch with some spray I had in my trunk to wipe off the scratch both on her car and on mine.

We talked for a bit, introduced ourselves to each other.

I then gently laid my hand on her shoulder, and as the Lord had asked me to do, I prayed for her. I was a bit surprised that she welcomed the prayer so easily as if she really needed it, so I knew that the command had come from God!

A few days later, her husband came to me as I was leaving for work and handed me a card, saying that his wife wanted me to have it as a thank you card. I thought it was sweet and opened it up. It was a Wall Mart card that read *"Gas and a whole lot more"*. That day I needed some gas and asked the Lord for provision. He provided!

Then He reminded me "I asked you to Pray for her and you did without question". I *BELIEVE* the Lord would have still provided... however, the timing was so perfect that there was no question in my mind that it was God answering my prayer and providing me with provision at just the "right" time!

14

The power to forgive

Several years ago The Lord walked me through the path of true forgiveness. Forgiving others. This is an extremely difficult area in my life, and although I have come a long way, it is NOT a Kingdom area that comes very easily for me.

There was presented to me a decent amount of money that I was made aware of by the attorney responsible for one of my parent's estate. One of the beneficiaries decided that the amount offered was not enough and we should look into possibly moving toward "litigation". This was against the decent counsel of our attorney, and all proceedings was halted, permanently.

This caused me great concern, not to mention embarrassment on my part as that was a "miracle" and a very timely and unexpected gift. The timing of it would have been perfect, and yet another blessing, it seemed was dashed to the floor. I spoke to my "pastor" about it, who prayed with me and though he brought healing in a physically manifested way, the yes that I was hoping for was not to be realized.

HORRIBLE.

Over the course of time I took steps to look deep within and ask God "HOW" *DO I FORGIVE THIS*. Realizing that I am not the only person in the world to experience forgiving another human being regardless of the offense they may cause me, I asked God for help. In the end, He, GOD is the only one that can supernaturally install "forgiveness" into your heart of flesh.

He did.

About 1 year later a friend asked me about the incident, and to my surprise, I had "no clue" what they was referring to, she literally had to refresh my memory. It was then that I realized that I had forgiven that offense, and forgiven that person.

I was healed! What a relief!

God thought it best to show me the art of forgiveness than to allow me the gift of unexpected funds. His inheritances are far more eternal than earthly inheritances, which are only temporary.

His Kingdom and redemption plan rests on forgiving others the way Jesus Christ forgives us.

It hurts.

But...

Sets you, the captive, free!

15

The anointing

There was a season in my life that I entered, where the love in my heart turned completely transfixed and intertwined with Jesus. I had stopped dancing or performing on stage for people and just began worshipping the Lord with abandon. I did not care about the thoughts or accolades of the audience.

ALL I cared about was Jesus and worshipping Him with the dance He placed inside of me. That was all I wanted. I would turn up the music and just dance around my bed in my bedroom just me and Jesus. Worshipping, crying, dancing, just He and I alone, it was ONLY for Him.

There were friends of mine that kept telling me that I had to dance again…one of those friends was admonishing me that I "should" dance and that it was a gift and all the rest of it! She was speaking of me dancing on stage, and that was over for me.

I began to question myself and wondered and pondered upon the Lord in true guidance as to what He wanted me to do. My other girlfriend was very persistent to the point of "wondering" why I had just stopped…I didn't tell anyone that I was in a sweet season of new wine worshipping the Lord and that my sweet worshipping moments were tender, raw, intimate, private, and wonderful. Engulfing me in every moment.

These were private times.

My girlfriend Deborah, a singer, quite beautiful herself and extremely gifted, asked me to dance for a small church in Atlanta, Georgia. I went to the Lord and had a talk with Him. I explained to the Lord that I didn't want to dance for recognition anymore to boost my ego strength anymore I just wanted to dance for Him….I didn't care what people thought …

I just DID NOT CARE!

I just wanted Him, that's ALL!! Just Him.

So I spoke with Him and said ok…"unless you anoint me with oil" I do not want to dance before people…my worship had now become private and intimate, untouchable by anyone else."

If you anoint me with oil then I will know that "You" approve of my dance and that I will be dancing for only "You."

I can be very stubborn you know.

Would these people please leave me alone with Jesus?

I promptly forgot about my conversation with Jesus and left it at that. My girlfriend Deborah persisted and persisted for weeks and months, for crying out LOUD leave me alone!

I relented

I danced at the small church to a song called "O Holy One."

I had not danced in a couple of years so my body needed a physical tune up but I danced none the less at their Sunday worship service.

The atmosphere was dripping with the Holy Ghost and I was enveloped in His abiding love and the felt presence of Angelic beings.

I could not leave the service after it was over as I was just soaking in His presence and just could not leave.

The pastor of the church asked one of the young men to have me come to the altar. My eyes were closed as I was now sitting in with the rest of the congregation.

I went up to the altar and the Pastor took a bottle of oil and poured it over my head.

As I sank to the floor in sweet submission.

It was then I remembered the conversation I had with the Lord some years before..

Unless you anoint me with oil ...I do not want to dance/perform anymore for people ...because I just wanted you.

I wept in wonder at His answer and His..

"Yes".

Some weeks after he (same pastor) smeared my son Adam with oil and set him aside.

I am forever grateful for God's grace and protection upon my life, my son's life and that of His of beautiful wife and family.

So thankful and humbled. I do not take the "oil" anointing of the Lord lightly as I learn how to move and dance with this gracious and precious mantle He has placed on me.

I am not concerned with looks of other people, their thoughts or whatever they may think when I dance.

This time is His and His alone. I am forever in wonder of how he gave me an answer when I completely forgot about the question and He said

"Yes"...

16

Birthday present

…car trouble!

Valentine Day I received a phone call from my "little" big brother Herb Jr.

I asked him why was he calling me on valentine's day? We laughed and proceeded with the real reason he was calling, to sell me a car.

The NERVE!!!

Anyway...

hold on, this turns out to be a beautiful testimony!!

His beautiful wife Tamara told him that she thought it was time I got a new car!

SHE WAS RIGHT!

He did what every dutiful and obedient husband would do said "yes dear"

So we started the process... He is exceptional at his job so I was in extraordinary hands.

I trusted him.

Meanwhile as I was waiting for the process to take due course I still drove my 1999 Saturn, Fred Flinstone style, the cartoon.

It soon came time for me to have my tags replaced on my old car..

That is when trouble began..

I failed my emissions test necessary to have the tags replaced and the car needed repair. With no real time as to when I would be getting my new car I had to proceed with getting the old car fixed.

I didn't have the extra funds to fix the old and place a proper down payment on the new, and time was running out!!

I was less than a week away from the legal deadline of my tags.

In frustration at the very last day I simply held the

FAILED

Emissions report up to the heavens and said to Jesus

"Fix It"

I wasn't rude or arrogant to the Lord, it was a cry of desperation!

I went back to my apartment and was doing some work on the PC when Herbie called,

"Hey! A Volvo just rolled up here when can you pick it up?" Can you come get it today?!

"What"!

"…excuse me".. less then 1 hour before I asked Jesus to "fix it"

The answer was rolling up into the car dealership as I was asking God to

"fix it"

I went in the next day got my new car and rolled out with an unexpected birthday gift! I got the car about a week before my birthday!! What a present

HE IS ALWAYS ON TIME.

OH BY THE WAY…VOLVOS ARE MY FAVORITE CARS.

17

Adam's prayer

2.2.06

Dear Lord,

- Please keep Adam away from sin and temptation If he becomes tempted-give him the wisdom to pray for a swift escape in order not to commit sin
- Keep all evil far from him – dispatch angels continually, all his warring angels that have been assigned to him since the foundation of the earth.
- Give him divine wisdom & discernment far beyond his years Lord – teach him understanding also and give him the will to want to use these gifts for your glory.
- Surround him – hedge around him – double hedge around him godly and "on fire" friends from God- friends that will only guide him to the truth about himself and about You
- Keep him always uplifted and keep depression far from him- keep favor surrounding him like a shield. Keep him in perfect peace that passes all understanding and his mind stayed on you Lord.

- Give him back his tender heart towards you Lord. Give him a divine desire to want to do only what is right and just – not lawless.
- Give him maturity and distinction Father in all his ways and in his walk. Remove peer pressure far from him – give him godly confidence. Teach him temperance and the fruits of the Spirit. Keep him clothed in meekness and humility – keep him divinely healthy and prosperous. Give him prudence Father and bring him back double to where he would be now had he not strayed. Recover and redeposit everything that was lost or stolen from him.
- Give him a godly, holy, virtuous and physically beautiful wife. Give him sweet, beautiful, kind, healthy children.
- Fulfill Your destiny for him Father. Turn his heart fiercely towards you.

His mommy

Kirsten

On Saturday June 9, 2018 at 11:18 PM this prayer was fully answered in its entirety.

…Is it 8'oclock yet….

18

2006... Sowing Seed

Sowing Seed during a time of famine.....

During a time of my life I was in a very difficult season with a most beloved and cherished member of my family. We were both under immense spiritual attack that ONLY PRAYER could quench, no human help could do the trick.

I spent the better part of four to five years trying to overcome this attack.

I would later learn that this attack came shortly after I produced a play that brought over 400 souls back to the Lord, so of course the enemy wasn't happy about that! So he attacked with witchcraft, finances, sickness, job loss, persecution, everything and I was sent into MAJOR warfare. As a growing and maturing Christian, at that time, my only weapon was to fight with everything I knew and had in my little arsenal bag.

PRAYER.

I was the only person my cherished family member had. I dropped EVERYTHING.

I moved, by faith, from my home to another home in another part of town, the enemy followed me there. The attack became stronger. The Holy Ghost lead me through some disciplines to follow which I did.

I woke up every morning from 4 AM until 7 AM and went to the prayer tower of the church I was a member of and prostrated myself before the Throne room and prayed every day for about a year. I would go home take a shower and go to work for 12 hours 6 days a week.

I lost my job, a decent paying job.

75K.

Lost

my car.

my home.

my mind.

During that time, before losing my job I received a bonus from my boss of 3K, I sowed 2K as a first fruit offering, ***during a time of famine,*** as Isaac sowed. I was expecting a return of 100 fold like Isaac received.

I forgot about the seed sown and simply kept battling and doing prophetic acts, without knowing they were prophetic...doing them simply because the bible said so.

During that time I became very close to the deliverance and healing pastor of that church and she and I battled for the soul of my most cherished and beloved son.

During /soaking/prayer one morning the manifest, felt presence of the Lord Jesus Christ entered the room. The music stopped when it usually kept playing.

It stopped.

Jesus stepped in.

In His presence is the fullness of joy.

The reverential fear of Lord and the Glory of the Lord was there. My tears and my breathing stopped. There was another prayer warrior with me. We were both amazed, and kept perfectly still. Jesus remained with us for about 5-8 minutes.

It was Jesus.

I know the difference between Jesus and angelic arrival, activity and presence.

In the presence of angels you are quiet.

In the presence of Jesus ...

You are ...

Transfixed.

On Sunday January 7, 2007 at 1:00 AM on a Sunday morning... in the wee hours of the morning my most cherished, and beloved son rededicated his life back to the Lord.

I was weak, and spent.

After years of strategic "home grown" war faring prayer, the fallow ground had been plowed up.

Several years later I asked the Lord two questions:

Just what kind of prayers did I send up there..

He responded.

The effectual fervent prayer of a righteous man avail much... kind of prayers.

What happened to that one hundredfold return on the two thousand dollars that I sowed?

He responded...

Adam.

19

...I Love You... !

A few years ago, a girlfriend and I wanted to get together for lunch, but found it hard to coordinate our schedules. Anyway, we were finally able to do so and we decided up on a date. I was so excited to meet with her one of my Best friends fore ever (BFF), I forgot to spend time with Jesus as it was my normal thing to do first thing in the morning.

When I realized this, I felt badly, and told Jesus that I was sorry as I was running out the door on my way to a happy day!

I said "Jesus I love you sooo much" and xoxooxox, as I ran down the staircase to my car!

I met my friend and her husband for lunch and had a fabulous time. They knew the General Manager of the restaurant who spoke with us and made us feel very special!

We asked for the check and told that everything was comped!

Wow! What a wonderful treat I thought! I got into my car I realized that God had paid for the check, and said...

"Jesus thank you so much for taking care of that for me"

He said..

"You did say you loved me!!!"

Wow...

I know a very simple thing, some of you, as you read this, may say "what's the big deal"

... I thought it was a sweet and big deal. Sometimes God just wants us to tell Him how much we love Him...that's all!

Pushing the envelope, I said

"Jesus, what are you doing for dinner??"

He said that money you saved for lunch, you can take it go to whole foods and buy yourself a "fine dinner", shaking His Head I am sure! I am such a little rascal!

Yes, I love Jesus Christ and Yes I love talking with Him and being a wonderful part of His Kingdom as He shows me more and more of His grace and mercy and being able to approach Him as a human being!

20

Kirsten's Prayer and Declaration

Dear LORD,

- Lord I know now is a **KAIROS** moment for "favor" "acceleration" "unusual occurrences" and "supernatural interventions". I ask you Father to give me specific favor with the production and increase of my Salad Dressing line / **K VINAIGRETTE**. Lord, please bring to fruition the screenplay of

"My heart belongs to Daddy/Tribute to Jesus".

I am asking for much ...but to **YOU** it is little.

You are the God of the impossible and more than enough. I dare to/ask/believe that you will give me favor in the time of favor, and to surround me with favor as with a shield, even now.

- I ask you for such a miraculous blessing that is so supernatural that peoples, enemies, persons, friends, family and relatives will know and notice that "you" Lord has done this work, in the working of miracles.

Cause me to walk under an open heaven.

- I would like to utilize the funds to bless your Kingdom and advance it the way you would want me to. That is all I have ever wanted to do is to bless the poor/needy and your Kingdom. Please do this for me. I also want to live financially debt free and unencumbered so that I am able to give and leave an inheritance for my children and my children's children.

- Thank you for healing me as much as You have so far, but I now ask for WHOLE DIVINE and TOTAL healing to be manifested in my life SUDDENLY and in this KAIROS moment. For my soul, spirit and physical body to be healed in all and every facet you created it to function. Your son, my savior, Jesus Christ died for this and the work He did by dying for me is a finished work, I believe this with all my heart.

- Father, please answer me quickly and suddenly, blow me away with your response to my request. I thank you in advance!

- I love you regardless, your "awaiting bride"

Kirsten.

Getting close to 8'Oclock

21

Tributes

My Father

Honor thy mother and thy father the first commandment with a promise.

I never saw my father hold a bible in his hands or necessarily go to church, however, I did see him live out the simple Gospel Jesus Christ.

He fleshed out the compassionate love of Christ walking always under an open heaven. He was blessed with a gift of *speed* in his feet and attained greatness on the world stage. He had what Eric Lidel spoke about in the film "Chariots of Fire". God had made him

"Fast"

..But that was not his true destiny, when he came to his beloved homeland he used the platform and access God gave him to help and love everyone…He was not perfect

Just showed perfected love to the helpless and downtrodden.

Yes he did… I saw many people jeer him and some didn't have nice things to say about him at times but he showed forgiveness to them anyway.

Forgiveness, it seemed, came easy for him. He had the access to the highest ranks in the government an d when he passed away there were four prime ministers of our country at his funeral three of whom spoke a "tribute" of the gentle man that He was.

It is under this beautiful and tender mantle that his children, grandchildren and great grandchildren walk under.

Before he died I had a prophetic dream about him where he had died in the dream but was brought back to life.

He left us this message.

"Carry on what I have begun"

He died that year.

I pray I carry on his legacy.

This I will do with all my heart.

My Mother, Ruth

Timeless beauty, brilliant, a hidden gem, prudent and wise. Loved her children with all her heart.

I love you Mummy, so very much, you are etched in the most sacred and sealed part of my heart.

Gone too soon.

Enjoy heaven!

Aunt Beverly

Faithful and true to the very end. She raised five children, of which only one was hers by natural birth.

Each of us, all five had very different personalities and needs.

Frankly, we were difficult, however, as our father's wife of forty years she was the stabilizing FORCE in our family. Aunt Beverly was ALWAYS there. It was Aunt Beverly, who came to be with me in the States when it was time to give birth to my son. She stayed with me for at least one month showing me how to breast feed him, when to feed him, when to bathe him. I needed help.

Now that I am much older and have grandchildren of my own, I have come to realize how strong and FAITHFUL she was to us, and her husband, our father.

I would like to take this time to honor Aunt Beverly for her genuine love towards us, her family.

I hold her with the highest love and honor and am grateful that I carry in my heart the compassionate love of Jesus Christ for her.

I love you,

Aunt Beverly.

EPILOGUE

As I process everything in my life, friends, enemies, family and whoever is in between. I realize that we are all the same struggling with ourselves, and each other. Some of us are wise enough to realize that earlier in their life, some not!

It takes a big heart to see the log in our eyes before committing to take the log out of another person's eye. We do not always succeed. Simply put, as I move forward I have come to know that LOVE is the only anecdote to correct ourselves, just as Jesus taught us.

It is very simple, just love. It is at times, easier to love someone from a distant…some close, some even closer. However, whatever we do just commit to love God, yourself and each other. Sounds easy enough, but MOST difficult to do.

In the end you truly find out that Jesus Christ is that friend that sticks

CLOSER

THAN

A Brother

LOVE

The Kingdom of Heaven love is the Love and compassion Jesus showed on the cross to the repentant man hanging on the cross beside Him asking for His forgiveness and Jesus having the capacity to love and forgive this man when He, Jesus was dying himself for our sins. His, Jesus' cup was running over enough to give of himself.

His LOVE capacity was more than enough to pour out, when it seems impossible ...that is what I am learning to ascribe to.

When you can honestly say..

Father forgive them because they know not what they do, you know that you have crossed over! True health and character are now part of your DNA and you have the mind of Christ, the scriptures start to become a part of you and the way you think.

Your thoughts begin with Christ first and His glorious love.

GOD *IS* LOVE.

Is it 8'O Clock yet?

Yes, it is 8 O Clock!

It did not come as I thought it would, when I was four years old waiting for the hands of the clock to move, it came another way.

Jesus.

He healed and set me free on the inside. He has made me whole and has imparted His joy unspeakable and full of glory. I could not say these words if they were not true. I am grateful that the Lord worked all things out for my good, and remains faithful to me every day.

Yes..

It

Is

8'O Clock.

Prayer of Salvation, for anyone who is willing.

Jesus I believe that you are the Son of God and that you died for me to save me from my sins. I ask you to forgive me of all my sins, cleanse me of all unrighteousness and heal my soul. Remove the hurt, pain, disease, both physical, and emotional.

Wash me with Your Blood that you bled and shed on that old rugged cross at Calvary.

Crucify my flesh, remove my heart of stone and replace it with a heart of flesh so that I can love the way you love.

Give me the eyes, ears, and heart of an innocent child. Create in me a new heart Lord, Jesus and a right spirit. Teach me your ways and speak to me your excellent counsel, mantle me with your Love.

I have fallen in love with you..

Jesus.

Printed in the United States
by Baker & Taylor Publisher Services